*Respectfully dedicated to
the Duke and Duchess of Cambridge
and Prince George.*

*And to proud parents everywhere
who have experienced a joyful debut
of their own little prince or princess.*

*May the jubilation of your child's birth
continue to fill your heart and your world
each and every day of your life.*

JACQUELINE

By Royal Order of the Palace,
It is now and hereby declared that

This joyful book shall forever belong to

_____.

It was given this

___ day of _____, 20 ___

by

_____.

I wish to thank attorney Jeanne Seewald for her professional assistance, thoughtful comments, and remarkable insight. Thank you also to Michael Biondo for his creative guidance, continuous friendship, and endless support. And a very heartfelt thank you to Naren Aryal for recognizing the potential of my work, indulging me throughout the process, and building a machine that magically transforms dreams into reality.

Honorable mention to Mascot team members:
Laura Falcon (project manager); Josh Taggert (graphic design); Josh Patrick (marketing and promotion); and Danny Moore (cover graphic).

This book was written to celebrate the royal birth in a way that respects and preserves the privacy of the family. Illustrations of the baby were created months before the birth and are not based on any likeness. It is my hope that children and families throughout the world will continue to feel the great joy of this momentous event for many years to come with each and every reading.

JACQUELINE

A Joyful Royal Debut: Presenting Prince George!

PRT0813A

Printed in the United States

ISBN-13: 9781620863053
ISBN-10: 1620863057

www.mascotbooks.com

A Joyful Royal Debut

Presenting Prince George!

JACQUELINE J. BUYZE

Illustrated by

ELISA MORICONI

It's a PRINCE!

Born 22 July 2013 at 4:24 pm

Weight: 8 lbs, 6 oz

Her Royal Highness and her
child are both doing well.

One day in December,
a glorious morn,
The palace announced
that a babe would be born.

A new Royal Highness
would soon be world-known.
The heir to the Queen
will accede to the Throne!

Proud father, Prince William, and mum-to-be, Kate,
Had found in each other a lifelong soul mate.

Their fairytale wedding and balcony kiss
Were just the beginning of newlywed bliss.

With hopes of a child, they were blessed from above
Expecting a baby conceived out of love.

The Queen was delighted. Her family was, too.
And as each day passed, an excited joy grew.

It spread throughout England and all through the land
As everyone passed along news that was grand.

It reached all of Europe
    and crossed every sea,
Uniting the world
    in a vast, joyful glee.

And then from the world,
    the joy started to rise
It drifted through treetops
    and up toward the skies.

It flowed to the sun,
    to the moon, and the stars.
It kept getting bigger
    and reached beyond Mars!

And with it, this joy brought a feeling of hope
To people who struggled and worked hard to cope.

The future seemed brighter than ever before
With thoughts of the royal whom all would adore.

With all eyes upon them, Prince William and Kate
Had much to prepare while awaiting the date.

They set up their nurseries with lovely decor,
And thrilled in this work that was never a chore.

The rooms they created were tranquil and sweet,
And from floor to ceiling, each one was complete.

They picked every pillow for cradle and bed
Just perfect for baby to lay down his head.

The warmest of blankets from fleece of a sheep.
The comfiest chairs made for rocking to sleep.

The prettiest pictures to hang on the wall.
The plushest of rugs to lie down on and crawl.

The cuddliest critters to hug and to shake,
And entertain baby when he is awake.

They found lovely lamps that would give gentle light,
just perfect for reading good books in the night.

As soon as they finished
and with things in place,
They held one another
in loving embrace.

Imagining how life with baby would start,
They knew precious moments would fill up their heart.

And then came the day
        the whole world waited for:
The birth of a new prince
        that all did adore.

A beautiful boy
        with an angelic face,
An infant so perfect
        and so full of grace.

Crowds started to cheer and bells joyously rang.
Guns used for saluting let out a big bang.

The baby was healthy and mother was, too,
And so they appeared for the royal debut!

Prince William, elated and beaming with pride,
Surrounded by family and Kate at his side.

All smiled as they waved, and with tears in their eyes,
Presented the newborn so tiny in size.

The Queen was ecstatic! Her family was, too.
And as each day passed, a euphoric joy grew.

It spread through Great Britain and throughout the land,
As everyone saw a new face that was grand.

It reached all of Europe and crossed every sea,
Uniting the world in a jubilant glee.

Then up from the world, jubilation did rise.
It tickled the treetops and lit up the skies.

It made the moon smile and it made the stars dance.
The world fell in love from the first moment's glance.

It's true that our world is a happier place.
The birth of this child put a smile on each face.

Events such as this are quite special and rare.
So when they occur, it is something we share.

A wonderful treasure, this child of the Throne,
Will wear the Crown Jewels one day when he is grown.

But now he just slumbers, sweet dreams fill his head.
With family near, he has nothing to dread.

His days will begin with an early sunrise
And each will be filled with wonder and surprise...

This short, little story is my gift to you.
I hope when you read it, you felt great joy, too.

Because, my dear reader, this book is the start
Of a Royal Series I wrote from my heart.

Jacqueline

The second book in the Royal Baby series is planned for
release in 2014. For more information, go to
www.RoyalBabyBooks.com.

Read! Share! Enjoy!

Succession to the Crown Act 2013

Historically, the Act gave preference in the Right of Succession to boys over girls. The law was recently amended to ensure that the firstborn child of Prince William, regardless of gender, would secure a place in the line of succession behind the Prince. This momentous change in law symbolizes a continued evolution to a more modern British Monarchy.

Jacqueline J. Buyze is an attorney, a professional speaker, and a freelance children's book writer. *A Joyful Royal Debut* is her third published book and the first in a series she has written in about the royal baby. With this series, Jacqueline hopes to share the joy of the birth and future auspicious royal occasions with all the world in a respectful way that preserves the privacy of the family, and most importantly, Prince George.

Jacqueline did not plan to become a children's book writer. She wrote her first book, entitled *A Story of Lawyers*™, to teach her nieces and nephews about the work she and her friends do as practicing attorneys. At the encouragement of colleagues and friends, the book was published and expanded into her first series. Jacqueline received her B.A. in psychology, cum laude, from the University of South Florida and her J.D. from Stetson University College of Law.

Jacqueline has resided in Naples, Florida, since 1986. Prior to attending law school, she enjoyed a ten-year career with the Ritz-Carlton Hotel.

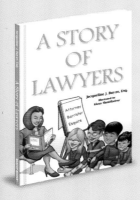

ISBN-10: 193740630X
ISBN-13: 9781937406301
Retail Price $14.95

A *Story of Lawyers*™ is a series of books originally written to teach the author's nieces and nephews about the important work lawyers do. With sensical rhyme and delightful illustration, the books provide a fun introduction to the practice of law that children of all ages will enjoy. A tribute to the profession, this series is a must-have for lawyers and educators and a must-read for clients, families, children, and students. The series is also a perfect supplement to any civics or law related education efforts. Available where books are sold.

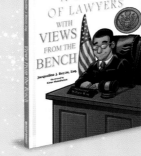

ISBN-10: 1620862530
ISBN-13: 9781620862537
Retail Price $14.95

For additional information about the author, books, subsequent titles, and release dates, please visit
www.aStoryOfLawyers.com
or
www.RoyalBabyBooks.com

LIKE the author on Facebook at
www.facebook.com/AuthorJacquelineBuyze

To schedule an appearance or book signing, please email
info@royalbabybooks.com.

Contact us at:

Mascot Books
560 Herndon Parkway
Suite 120
Herndon, VA 20170

info@mascotbooks.com | www.mascotbooks.com